Collins English Readers

Amazing Aviators

Level 2
CEF A2–B1

Text by
F.H. Cornish

Series edited by
Fiona MacKenzie

Collins

HarperCollins Publishers
77–85 Fulham Palace Road
Hammersmith London W6 8JB

10 9 8 7 6 5 4 3 2 1

Original text
© The Amazing People Club Ltd

Adapted text
© HarperCollins Publishers Ltd 2014

ISBN: 978-0-00-754495-0

Collins® is a registered trademark of
HarperCollins Publishers Limited

www.collinselt.com

A catalogue record for this book is available
from the British Library

Printed in the UK by Martins the Printers

These readers are based on original texts
(BioViews®) published by The Amazing
People Club group.® BioViews® and The
Amazing People Club® are registered
trademarks and represent the views of the
author.

BioViews® are scripted virtual interview
based on research about a person's life and
times. As in any story, the words are only
an interpretation of what the individuals
mentioned in the BioViews® could have
said. Although the interpretations are
based on available research, they do not
purport to represent the actual views of
the people mentioned. The interpretations
are made in good faith, recognizing that
other interpretations could also be made.
The author and publisher disclaim any
responsibility from any action that readers
take regarding the BioViews® for educational
or other purposes. Any use of the BioViews®
materials is the sole responsibility of the
reader and should be supported by their own
independent research.

Cover image © Graeme Dawes/Shutterstock

♦ CONTENTS ♦

Introduction	4
Joseph-Michel Montgolfier	7
Louis Blériot	19
Charles Lindbergh	31
Amelia Earhart	45
Amy Johnson	59
Glossary	73

✦ Introduction ✦

Collins Amazing People Readers are collections of short stories. Each book presents the life story of five or six people whose lives and achievements have made a difference to our world today. The stories are carefully graded to ensure that you, the reader, will both enjoy and benefit from your reading experience.

You can choose to enjoy the book from start to finish or to dip in to your favourite story straight away. Each story is entirely independent.

After every story a short timeline brings together the most important events in each person's life into one short report. The timeline is a useful tool for revision purposes.

Words which are above the required reading level are underlined the first time they appear in each story. All underlined words are defined in the glossary at the back of the book. Levels 1 and 2 take their definitions from the *Collins COBUILD Essential English Dictionary* and levels 3 and 4 from the *Collins COBUILD Advanced English Dictionary*.

To support both teachers and learners, additional materials are available online at www.collinselt.com/readers.

The Amazing People Club®

Collins Amazing People Readers are adaptations of original texts published by The Amazing People Club. The Amazing People Club is an educational publishing house. It was founded in 2006 by educational psychologist and management leader Dr Charles Margerison and publishes books, eBooks, audio books, iBooks and video content which bring readers 'face to face' with many of the world's most inspiring and influential characters from the fields of art, science, music, politics, medicine and business.

◆ The Grading Scheme ◆

The Collins COBUILD Grading Scheme has been created using the most up-to-date language usage information available today. Each level is guided by a brand new comprehensive grammar and vocabulary framework, ensuring that the series will perfectly match readers' abilities.

		CEF band	Pages	Word count	Headwords
Level 1	elementary	A2	64	5,000–8,000	approx. 700
Level 2	pre-intermediate	A2–B1	80	8,000–11,000	approx. 900
Level 3	intermediate	B1	96	11,000–15,000	approx. 1,100
Level 4	upper intermediate	B2	112	15,000–18,000	approx. 1,700

For more information on the Collins COBUILD Grading Scheme, including a full list of the grammar structures found at each level, go to www.collinselt.com/readers/gradingscheme.

Also available online: Make sure that you are reading at the right level by checking your level on our website (www.collinselt.com/readers/levelcheck).

Joseph-Michel Montgolfier

• ♦ •

1740–1810

the man who helped humans to fly

All my life, I was an <u>inventor</u>. I designed the first hot-air balloons. My brother Étienne and I made it possible for humans to fly through the air.

◆ ◆ ◆

I was born on 26th August 1740, in Annonay, in the Ardèche region of central France. My father, Pierre, owned a company which made paper in the town. My mother, Anne, gave Pierre 16 children, and I was the twelfth of them. When I was young, I was especially close to my brother, Jacques-Étienne. Étienne – we all called him that – was the fifteenth child. He was five years younger than me, but we were interested in the same things. In later years we worked together.

When we were children, Étienne and I often watched birds flying. 'Perhaps people could learn to fly too,'

I sometimes thought. I had the mind of an inventor at an early age, and people called me a <u>dreamer</u>. I certainly <u>dreamed</u> about flying. Étienne's mind was more <u>practical</u> than mine. While most of us stayed in Annonay, he moved to Paris. There, he studied to become an architect. However, he returned to us in 1772 when our eldest brother, Raymond, died. Raymond had been the <u>manager</u> of the family's paper-making <u>business</u>, after my father's <u>retirement</u>. Now Étienne took that job.

Étienne was a very successful <u>businessman</u>, and as a result, our family became rich. But my interest in inventing things was strong. Many people thought that my ideas were strange, but I didn't listen to them. Fortunately, Étienne didn't listen to them either.

In 1777, I had my first practical idea about human flight. One day, I was drying some <u>cloth</u> over a fire. I noticed that the cloth was moving. The hot air from the fire was lifting parts of it. I knew then that hot air was lighter than cold air, so I asked myself a question. Could hot air inside something that was heavier than air lift that thing off the ground? It was an idea that stayed in my mind.

In 1782, I was living in Avignon. I was interested in military planning at that time. I started to think about flying soldiers. Why was the idea of flying soldiers a good one? There were several reasons. For example, a soldier could fly over a battlefield. He could look down and see where his enemy's soldiers were. That could help his own army. Or perhaps the soldiers themselves could attack their enemy from the air.

I remembered my idea about using hot air to make something fly, and I shared it with my brother. We agreed that the main difficulty was the fire. The air inside a flying machine had to be hot. It had to be lighter than the air around the machine. So we needed to make something which could fly, but which contained a fire. The fire had to burn safely. We didn't want it to burn the machine.

I started to make <u>experiments</u>. One day, I made a wooden frame with the shape of a box. It was about one metre by one metre by one metre in size. I covered the frame with cloth on five sides, but I didn't cover the bottom of the box. I placed the box on a metal <u>stand</u> and I made a fire under it.

My experiment was a success. The box – the balloon, as I called it – started to rise from the ground. Was this a kind of flying machine? Yes it was! I was indoors at that time, so the machine soon hit the ceiling, but I saw that my idea was practical. It was time to build a larger machine and take it outside.

I wrote to my brother. I asked him to get lots more cloth and some <u>rope</u>. He quickly did this, and he came to Avignon and joined me in my work. I told him that he was going to see something amazing.

On 4th December 1782, our first outdoor balloon was ready. It was a very basic balloon, about three times as large as the first one. No one could fly in that balloon.

I wanted to <u>demonstrate</u> to people what could be done in the future. A large crowd came to see what was going to happen. Amazingly, the balloon <u>ascended</u>, and floated through the air for nearly two kilometres.

The next year, 1783, was the most important time for our work. We made a new balloon, which was larger than the second one. It had thick paper inside the cloth. This balloon held 790 <u>cubic metres</u> of air, and it weighed 225 kilograms. On 4th June that year, we gave a public <u>demonstration</u> of this balloon at Annonay. People from the government came to watch. 'Will the balloon leave the ground?' everyone wondered. We were happy when the demonstration succeeded. The flight lasted ten minutes, and the balloon reached an <u>altitude</u> of about 2000 metres above the ground. Like the second balloon, it <u>landed</u> about two kilometres from where it left the ground.

So, a machine could fly! We already knew that, but most of the people at the demonstration were amazed. News of our success moved faster than the balloon travelled. Soon, Étienne went to Paris to demonstrate our <u>invention</u> there. I was always a shy person and I decided to stay at home.

◆ ◆ ◆

11th September was the date of Étienne's first demonstration in the French capital city. Jean-Baptiste Réveillon, another man whose company made and sold

paper, helped my brother to make the new balloon. The flight started in Reveillon's garden. This balloon had a name – it was called *Aérostat Réveillon*. The signs of the <u>zodiac</u> were painted on it. Everyone thought that it looked wonderful.

On that occasion, the king, Louis the Sixteenth, had told Étienne that two <u>criminals</u> could fly in the basket – the <u>compartment</u> for <u>passengers</u> at the bottom of the balloon. We wanted to test the effects of flight on living things, because we wanted our balloons to carry men and women in the future. But Étienne said that criminals didn't deserve the <u>honour</u>.

However, a week after that flight, another flight took place at the Royal Palace in Versailles. This time, a sheep, a duck and a chicken were in the basket. The date was 19th September, and a huge crowd came to watch the flight. King Louis and Queen Marie-Antoinette themselves were there, and again the flight was successful. This time, the balloon travelled about three kilometres in eight minutes. It flew at about 500 metres above the ground. None of the animals was hurt.

Immediately, Étienne built a huge new balloon which held 1,700 cubic metres of air. It was about 24 metres high, and about 16 metres wide. The king's face, as well as the zodiac signs, was painted on this balloon. On 15th October, in this balloon, my brother became the first human to ascend into the air. It was a tethered flight – the balloon was tied to the ground with a very long rope. This was because we still needed a way to control the balloon's direction of flight.

Later that same day, another man ascended in the machine. He was called Jean-François Pilâtre de Rozier, and after that day he flew in Étienne's balloons on a number of occasions.

Soon, Étienne decided that the tether-rope wasn't necessary. The balloon could fly untethered in future. On 21st November, the marquis d'Arlandes – who was a famous soldier – and monsieur Pilâtre de Rozier made the first untethered flight. Monsieur de Rozier controlled the balloon's direction on that day. So you could say that he was the world's first pilot! The two men flew over Paris. They reached an altitude of 900 metres and they stayed in the air for 25 minutes. Parisians were amazed to see the balloon sailing across the sky.

That flight had a moment of danger. A piece of hot wood jumped from the fire and started to burn the cloth. The pilot had to land the balloon quickly. But no one was hurt and everyone was happy that the two aviators had returned safely to Earth.

◆ ◆ ◆

Much more work was needed to improve the balloons. Étienne and I made many more experiments. The *Académie des Sciences* recognized our achievements. However, our work was interrupted by the French <u>Revolution</u>.

In 1789, the streets of Paris were dangerous places, especially for the rich people. <u>Survival</u> in the streets became more important than survival in the air, so we stopped flying. But we'd shown that human flight was possible. We'd changed the way people thought about travel.

Soon after our machines first flew, other inventors started to make balloons which were filled with hydrogen, not hot air. Hydrogen, a gas which had recently been discovered, was lighter than air. It didn't need to be heated. But balloons continued to be people's only way of flying, long after my own death on 26th June 1810. It was almost a hundred years later when a different kind of flying machine moved the history of aviation forward again.

The Life of Joseph Montgolfier

1740   Joseph-Michel Montgolfier was born in Annonay, Ardèche, France. He was the twelfth child of 16 born to his parents. The Montgolfier family were paper-makers.

1745   Joseph's brother Jacques-Étienne (always called Étienne) was born.

1760   Joseph completed his education and began to work in the family's paper-making business.

1772   Étienne, Joseph's brother, returned from Paris where he had studied architecture. He managed the family business after the death of their older brother.

1777   Joseph began to talk about ideas for a flying machine with Étienne. He thought that a machine could fly with the help of hot air.

1782   While living in Avignon, Joseph began building the first hot-air balloon. When his brother joined him in the work, they built a larger balloon which flew two kilometres.

1783   In Annonay the brothers made the first public demonstration of their hot-air balloon. The flight was a success and the balloon flew two kilometres in ten minutes. Next, they made another hot-air balloon called the *Aérostat Réveillon*. Its first flight was successful and soon there was another demonstration at the Royal Palace of Versailles. King Louis XVI and Queen Marie-Antoinette watched as the balloon ascended. A month later, Étienne made the first successful human flight in a tethered balloon.

1789–1799   The French Revolution ended the Montgolfier brothers' work on balloons for several years. Joseph and Étienne returned to the family paper-making business. But after the Revolution they continued their work on inventions. Soon, hot-air balloons were replaced by hydrogen balloons. But Joseph invented several important machines of other kinds.

1810   Joseph died aged 69, in Balaruc-les-Bains.

Louis Blériot

• ◆ •

1872–1936

the first person to cross the sea in an aeroplane

I was the first person to cross the sea from France to England in a <u>heavier-than-air</u> flying machine.

◆ ◆ ◆

I was born in the town of Cambrai, in France, on 1st July 1872. I went to school in my home town, then in Amiens, and finally in Paris. As a boy, I was especially good at drawing. My ambition was to become an <u>engineer</u>.

When I left the famous École Centrale in Paris, I had to join the French Army. All young men had to do some military service at that time, and I was a soldier for a year. After that, I took a job with an <u>engineering</u> company in Paris. While I was working there, I <u>invented</u> something new. It was a <u>practical</u> kind of <u>headlamp</u> for the first cars which were appearing in France at that time.

In 1897, I left the engineering company and I started a company of my own. I sold my headlamps to famous car makers like Renault. My company was successful and in 1901, I was able to marry a beautiful woman called Alice Védères.

◆ ◆ ◆

I'd been interested in aviation when I was a student. But during the Great Exhibition in Paris in 1900, my interest became stronger. At the exhibition, I saw a kind of aeroplane called *Avion Three*. It had been built by an <u>inventor</u> named Clément Ader. That machine didn't succeed in flying, but it made *me* think about flying machines. My headlamp company was earning a lot of money, so I used some of it to build aeroplanes myself.

My ambition was to make heavier-than-air machines which could fly. I wanted machines that didn't need gas inside them. Fortunately, small, light engines had recently been invented. My machines needed engines like that, I thought. One of my first designs, in 1900, was a machine which I called the 'ornithopter'. I made several of these machines. The ornithopter had engines and it was meant to fly like a bird, with wings which moved. Unfortunately, none of the machines worked.

They didn't work because the design was wrong. The moving wings were a mistake. So next, I started to think about <u>fixed-wing</u> aeroplanes. Perhaps the <u>movement</u> of the air over the fixed wings could keep an aeroplane in the sky.

I <u>established</u> a company with a man named Gabriel Voisin. Voisin had already worked on fixed-wing aeroplanes, but they were gliders. These aeroplanes had no engines, so they had to <u>take off</u> from high places. Now we needed to make machines with engines to pull them forward and pull them up into the sky.

In 1905 and 1906, Voisin and I built several aeroplanes. By this time, the Wright brothers in America had already flown in heavier-than air flying machines with engines. But the machines that I built with Voisin didn't work well. The pilots who tried to fly them weren't happy. They said that the machines were dangerous.

I was wasting my money while I was working with Voisin. Soon, I left the company and I started working alone again. The result was the first successful <u>monoplane</u>. The monoplane had a single wing. It wasn't like the biplane – the two-winged design that the Wright brothers used.

I built several monoplanes, each one with changes to its design. And from each machine I learned something new. The *Blériot Five* model, for example, flew a short distance, but it was <u>unstable</u> and it crashed. But when I built model eleven, I'd solved most of the problems. This model was much more <u>stable</u> in the air.

My new aeroplane could fly, but how far could it travel? Could it cross the English Channel – the sea between England and France? This was my ambition.

People had flown across the Channel in balloons, of course. This had first happened in 1784. But it was the gas inside the balloons that kept them in the air. My <u>dream</u> was to fly from France to England in a heavier-than-air machine. Many people told me that it wasn't possible, but their doubts made me work harder.

The English Channel is about 35 kilometres wide at the narrowest place. That isn't very far. But until 1909, it was difficult to keep our aeroplanes in the air for more than a few minutes. However, in that year, I thought that my newest machine could succeed. There was one way to find out whether I was right.

There was a good reason to make the attempt then. A London newspaper, *The Daily Mail*, had offered a prize of £1,000. The money was for the first person whose aeroplane made the crossing. There were two other people competing for the prize. One of them had already made his first attempt. His engine had failed and he'd <u>landed</u> in the sea. Fortunately, he was rescued. The other competitor's aeroplane crashed during a test flight, and he was hurt.

On 25th July 1909, when I was ready to make my own attempt, I was in pain. I'd recently crashed one of my aeroplanes and burned my foot. The pain was bad, but I decided to fly that day. I took off from an airfield in

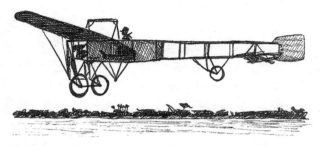

The Bleriot XI aeroplane which Louis Blériot flew across the English Channel

France at about 4.30 in the morning. I needed to <u>ascend</u> quickly because there were some <u>telegraph wires</u> at the end of the field. I had to get my machine safely above them. My aeroplane had a 25-<u>horsepower</u> engine. Was that enough? I hoped that it was.

The <u>take-off</u> was good, and soon I was flying over the water at about 70 kilometres per hour. But the weather changed, and it was hard to see anything around me. To be safe, I flew my machine about 75 metres above the water. It seemed a long time before I saw the English coast below me. But in fact, the whole flight took just 37 minutes.

It was good to see the English airfield ahead of me. The strong wind made it hard to land my machine. I decided to stop my engine and float down to earth. Because of this, I didn't have much control of the aeroplane, and I touched the ground hard. The machine was damaged a little as a result, but I'd succeeded. I'd flown across the Channel!

◆ ◆ ◆

I continued to design aeroplanes during the next years, and in 1914, they became much more important. That year, the First World War began. Britain and France both fought against Germany. By then, I was the director of a large aeroplane company and I had built over 800 machines. Although the technology was still new, and there were many crashes, aeroplanes were very useful during the war.

I moved my company to England during the war, and I stayed there for some years after it. We built cars as well as aeroplanes. I started several flying-schools in England too. But when I was in my 50s, I decided to retire. After that, although I stopped flying, my interest in aviation continued. It was good to see other pilots break records, and attempt long flights for the first time. In 1927, Charles Lindbergh crossed the Atlantic Ocean, flying alone, and I was in France to welcome him when he landed. And I continued to advise governments about military aviation until my death in Paris, on 1st August 1936. In that year, the *Fédération Aéronautique Internationale* established the Louis Blériot Medal, in my honour.

The Life of Louis Blériot

1872   Louis Charles Joseph Blériot was born in Cambrai, France.

1882   At the age of ten, he was went to live at his school – the *Institut Notre Dame* in Cambrai. During that time, he won many prizes, including one for his drawings.

1887–1896   Louis moved to a school in Amiens, and took courses in Science and German. Next he studied for a year at the *Collège Sainte-Barbe*, in Paris. And after that, Louis was accepted by the *École Centrale* in Paris, where he studied engineering for three years. After he left college, he did military service for a year. At the end of that time, he joined an electrical company, called Bagues, in Paris. He developed the first practical headlamps for cars.

1897   Louis established his own company. He made headlamps for famous car companies, like Renault and Panhard–Levassor.

1900   His interest in aviation led him to design his ornithopters.

1901   Louis married Alice Védères.

1905   Gabriel Voisin, who built gliders, decided to work with Louis to design some new models. The company that the two men established built two machines with engines.

1906   Louis and Gabriel decided to stop working together.

1907   Louis established another company and built more aeroplanes. The first successful monoplane was the *Blériot Seven*, which made two flights of more than 500 metres.

1908   In the *Blériot Eight*, Louis flew a 28-kilometre journey from Toury to Arteny and back.

1909   In the *Blériot Eleven*, Louis flew with other people in his aeroplane for the first time. He became the first person to fly an aeroplane across the English Channel and was given £1,000 as a prize. He also established a new world speed-record at the *Grande Semaine d'Aviation* at Reims.

1910   Louis was hurt when he crashed in Istanbul. Over the next few years, Louis built over 800 aircraft.

1913   With some other men, Louis bought the aeroplane company called the *Société pour les Appareils Deperdussin* and he became president of the company.

1914   The First World War began. Louis established flying schools in Britain, and his company built the *SPAD S.Thirteen* military aeroplanes.

1918   Louis established the Air Navigation and Engineering Company, in Addlestone, Surrey, England. The company made light aircraft and also *Blériot Whippet* cars.

1927   Louis was at Le Bourget airfield in Paris to welcome Charles Lindbergh, after his successful flight across the Atlantic.

1936   Louis died aged 64, in Paris, France. In the same year, the *Fédération Aéronautique Internationale* established the Louis Blériot Medal, in his honour.

Charles Lindbergh

◆ ◆

1902–1974

the man who flew in *The Spirit of Saint Louis*

When I flew alone and without stopping across the Atlantic Ocean, I became one of the most famous people in the world. But my life after that wasn't always a happy one.

◆ ◆ ◆

I was born in Detroit, in the USA, on 4th February 1902. My father was politician – he was a member of the American government. My mother was a schoolteacher. From an early age I was interested in flying.

After I left high school, I studied at an <u>engineering</u> college. However, I really wanted to be a pilot, so after two years, I left the college. I trained to be a pilot in Lincoln, Nebraska. My father lent me some money to buy my first aircraft. It was called *Curtiss Jenny* and I was able to practice flying in it. I was also able to use it to earn

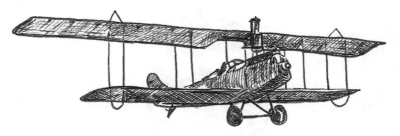

A Lincoln Standard biplane. Charles Lindbergh learned to fly in one of these.

some money – I took people for <u>pleasure-flights</u> in it. I did some stunt flying as well – I did dangerous tricks in the air while crowds of people watched from the ground.

In 1924, I joined the American Army <u>Reserve</u>, and completed some more training with them. Then late the next year, I started work at the Robertson Aircraft Company. My job was to fly mail between cities.

Being a mail pilot was dangerous work. One night, in a storm, my aircraft <u>ran out of</u> fuel and I had to jump out of it before it crashed. Fortunately, my <u>parachute</u> saved my life. But that was the kind of <u>risk</u> that all pilots took in those days.

I was one pilot among many until I decided to compete for the Orteig Prize. That was the most important decision of my early life. A rich <u>businessman</u> called Raymond Orteig had offered a prize of $25,000. The prize was for the first person to fly alone – and non-stop – between New York City and Paris, France. Orteig first offered the prize in 1919. By 1926, when I became interested in competing, no one had been able to win the money.

Several people had tried, and some of them had died as a result. I promised myself that I was going to succeed.

◆ ◆ ◆

I wasn't the first person to fly across the Atlantic Ocean. In fact, 81 people had done it before I did. But no one had done it non-stop and *alone*. Of course, crossing that huge ocean was dangerous even with a <u>co-pilot</u>. But with another pilot in the machine, the risk of falling asleep and crashing was not a big problem. However, I wanted to make the attempt, and I borrowed some money to pay for it. I had an aircraft built specially by the Ryan Aircraft Company. It was a <u>monoplane</u>, and I called it *The Spirit of Saint Louis*.

On 20th May 1927, I <u>took off</u> from Roosevelt Field, Long Island, New York City, and soon I was over the ocean. My aircraft had 1,704 litres of fuel. Apart from that, there were four sandwiches and two large bottles of water for my meals.

The flight lasted for more than 33 hours. Below me, nearly all the time, I could see the Atlantic Ocean. And several times I had to fly through storms. Sometimes there was <u>fog</u> in the air and it was necessary to fly very close to the waves. At other times, I could see <u>icebergs</u> floating silently below me in the ocean.

During the night, it was very cold in the <u>cockpit</u> of *The Spirit of Saint Louis.* I kept the windows open because the cold air helped me to stay awake. The noise of my engine was the only sound that I could hear. But while I could hear my engine, I knew that I was safe.

At last, I <u>landed</u> at Le Bourget airport, near Paris. More than 150,000 people came to watch my arrival. The French President gave me a <u>medal</u>, and of course I had won the Orteig Prize. After much celebration in France, I returned to the USA and on 13th June 1927, the people of New York City welcomed me home. The American President gave me some medals too. A few weeks before this, I had been an unknown mail pilot. Now suddenly, I was very famous – I was a celebrity.

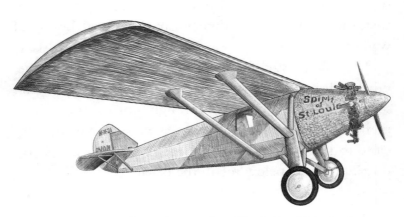

Charles Lindbergh's Ryan monoplane, The Spirit of Saint Louis

◆ ◆ ◆

Soon, I started on a tour of the USA. In three months, *The Spirit of Saint Louis* took me to 92 cities. In each place I made speeches, and there were many articles about me in newspapers. I also published a book about flying. Suddenly, more people wanted to invest money in aviation, and that was good for the aircraft builders.

Navigation in the air was a subject that I thought about a lot at that time. I was especially interested in mapping the route over the North Pole. Flying that route became my next big adventure. Again, it was a solo flight, so I had to be my own navigator. I spent many hours preparing for the trip. Fortunately, that flight was successful too.

◆ ◆ ◆

One day, while I was in Mexico making speeches for the American Government, I met a young lady called Anne Morrow. We fell in love, and on 27th May 1929, we were married. Anne wanted to become a pilot herself. I taught her to fly, and she soon became my aviation partner. We mapped several new routes together. One of them was the route across the North Pacific Ocean to China.

In 1930, my first son − Charles Augustus Lindbergh the Third − was born. Anne and I were very happy with our little boy, and we enjoyed seeing him grow. But on 1st March 1932, he was kidnapped from our home in

New Jersey. Suddenly our happiness disappeared. For ten weeks, we searched for him, and helped the police with *their* search. But, on 12th May, the police gave us the news that we'd feared. Little Charles was dead. Someone had killed him.

Time passed, and we had a second son, called John. 'Will someone try to kidnap him too?' we asked ourselves. We realized that we were frightened and unhappy in the USA. So at the end of 1935, we went to live in Britain. Our plans were secret, and we left America quietly to start a new life in Europe. I no longer wanted to be famous. I just wanted to enjoy my family. Over the next years, Anne and I had four more children.

Anne and I travelled a lot. We visited India and we travelled in various European countries. We wanted to find out what life was like for the people there. Then in 1938, the American army asked me to report on aviation in Germany. I told them that the German Air Force was very strong.

When I returned to Britain, I found that political views there were very mixed. Some people thought that Britain couldn't avoid fighting Germany. Others thought that Britain could avoid a war. But everyone agreed that the army in the UK wasn't prepared for a war. I told the American government that the German army could easily <u>invade</u> other countries. And I said that Britain and France could not stop them.

When the Second World War started in 1939, I took my family back to the USA. I made speeches about the need for a strong American Army. But I was against helping Britain fight the Germans. I said that Europeans needed to solve their own problems. I wasn't a popular person in my own country when I said this. But when Japan attacked the USA at Pearl Harbor in 1941, I changed my views. America entered the war and I began to advise the government about aviation. I also worked as a pilot.

After the war, I continued to advise the American Air Force. I advised the airline Pan Am as well. And in 1953, I wrote a book called *The Spirit of Saint Louis*. It told the story of my solo flight across the Atlantic. Many thousands of copies were sold, and the following year it won the Pulitzer Prize.

The later years of my life were spent on the island of Maui, in Hawaii. While I was there, I wrote my last book, *Autobiography of Values*. In that book I wrote about conservation ideas. I was especially interested in protecting whales. My last days were peaceful and I died in Maui on 26th August 1974.

THE SPIRIT OF
ST LOUIS

CHARLES A. LINDBERGH

The Life of Charles Lindbergh

1902   Charles Augustus Lindbergh was born in Detroit, Michigan, USA. His father, Charles August Lindbergh was a lawyer and a politician. His mother, Evangeline Lodge Land Lindbergh, was a teacher.

1918   Charles finished studying at Little Falls High School, in Minnesota.

1920   He began to study engineering at the University of Wisconsin, in Madison.

1922   Charles left the university. He trained to be a pilot and flew solo for the first time.

1923   At the age of 21, Charles earned his pilot's licence. His father borrowed some money to buy Charles his first aircraft, *Curtiss Jenny*.

1924   Charles joined the Army Air Service. He finished studying at the Advanced Flying School. And soon after that, he began work as a pilot in St Louis. He flew mail around the country.

1926   Charles decided to compete for the Orteig Prize. The prize of $25,000 was for the first aviator to fly non-stop from New York to Paris. Charles continued to work as a mail pilot. On 16th September, Charles's plane crashed, after he got lost in a storm. Fortunately, Charles wasn't badly hurt.

1927   Charles's new plane, *The Spirit of St Louis*, was built by the Ryan Aeronautical Company at San Diego in California. Charles took the plane on many test flights. On 12th May, he flew it across the United States to New York, in less than 22 hours. And soon after that, he flew it across the Atlantic. Later in the year, Charles met Anne Morrow.

1929   Charles married Anne Morrow.

1930   Charles and Anne's first baby, Charles Lindbergh Jnr, was born. The couple later had five more children.

1932   On 1st March, young Charles was kidnapped from the Lindberghs' home. His body was found around ten weeks later.

1935   Charles moved his family to England.

1938   The family moved again, to the Île Illiec in France.

1939   The family returned to the United States. Charles made speeches against the Americans joining the war. He didn't want his country to fight in the war which was beginning in Europe.

1941   Charles began working with Henry Ford, building bombers. He changed his views about the Second World War when Japan attacked America at Pearl Harbor.

1947   Charles began advising the US Air Force.

1948   Charles's book, *Of Flight and Life*, was published.

1953   His book, *The Spirit of St Louis* was published. The following year, the book won the Pulitzer Prize.

1964   After he became interested in conservation, Charles's article, *Is Civilization Progress?* was published in a magazine.

1969   He began building a house on Maui, in Hawaii. He lived there for the rest of his life.

1974   Charles died aged 72, in Maui, Hawaii.

Amelia
Earhart

◆ ◆ ◆

1897–1937

the woman who flew alone across the Atlantic

I was the first woman to fly alone across the Atlantic Ocean. After that, I broke many flying <u>records</u>. But flying was always a dangerous job. A crash in 1937 ended my career and my life at the age of 39.

◆ ◆ ◆

I was born in Atchison, in Kansas, USA, on 24th July 1897. My father was a lawyer who worked for a railway company. Our family lived in Kansas until 1907, when we moved to Iowa. We moved because my father took a new job there.

I was with my father when I saw an aircraft for the first time. That was in 1908, only five years after the first <u>heavier-than-air</u> machines had flown. The owner of the aircraft offered to take people for short <u>pleasure-flights</u>. My father asked me if I wanted to take a flight with him.

I looked at the aircraft, which was made of wood and <u>wire</u> and <u>cloth</u>. It looked very dangerous to me, so I didn't accept the offer.

In 1915, our family moved to Chicago, and I finished high-school there the next year. In that year, 1916, most of Europe was fighting in the First World War. America wasn't fighting that year, but Canada was fighting with Britain against Germany. When I visited Canada that year, I visited an army hospital.

The soldiers in the hospital were badly hurt. Their bodies were injured, but often their minds were injured too. Men had lost arms and legs. And men had lost their memories and their wish to live. I wanted to help these people, so I trained to be a nurse's assistant.

♦ ◆ ♦

One day, after the war ended in 1918, I went to a flying <u>display</u> with a friend. A pilot who had flown in the war did some stunt flying. He flew very low over our heads in his little red aircraft and did dangerous tricks. This time, I thought the flying machine looked exciting, not dangerous. It seemed to speak to me as it flew over us. I remembered that aircraft for many years afterwards.

The next year, I had a serious health problem. My <u>sinuses</u> became <u>infected</u>. As a result, I had bad headaches – pains in my head. During the next few years, I needed <u>surgery</u> on my sinuses. This happened several times, but the surgery didn't help much.

My parents decided to move to California. One day, when I was staying with them, my father asked me to go to an air display with him. The date was 28th December 1920, and that was a day that changed my life. A pilot called Frank Hawks offered to take me on a pleasure-flight. The flight lasted for only ten minutes, but by the time the aircraft had reached a height of 70 metres, I knew that flying was my future. I also knew that I needed money for flying lessons. In fact, I needed $1,000. My mother gave me some of the money.

My first flying lesson was at Kinner Field, near Long Beach. Anita Snook was my flying teacher. She was one of the first American woman aviators. Flying at that time was still a new and dangerous <u>hobby</u>, but I enjoyed my lessons. Within six months I'd bought my own aircraft. It was a <u>second-hand</u> Kinner Airster biplane, which I called *The Canary*.

On 22nd October 1922, I flew my aircraft to a height of 4,300 metres. That was a new world record for <u>altitude</u> by a female pilot. Soon there were other flights, and in May 1923, I earned my pilot's licence. So I was a qualified pilot, but not a very experienced one. Pilots with more experience sometimes warned me about taking <u>risks</u>. They thought that I was careless, and perhaps they were right.

In 1924, my headaches became very bad again. They were so bad that I had to stop flying. I sold my aircraft and I bought a car. I called the car *The Yellow Peril*, because of its colour. My mother and I drove across the USA in that car. We drove from Los Angeles to Boston.

In Boston, I had surgery on my sinuses again. This time, the surgery was successful. I was able to fly again, although I often had headaches. In fact, I had headaches for the rest of my life.

In 1927, Charles Lindbergh became famous when he flew non-stop, and alone, across the Atlantic Ocean. He was the first pilot to do that. Suddenly, Americans started to think, 'We can go anywhere'. And suddenly, everyone who cared about aviation was excited about flight across the Atlantic. 'Who will be the first woman to do it?' we all wondered.

One famous woman pilot, Amy Phipps Guest, was asked to make the attempt. She thought that the risks were too great and she refused. But she offered to pay for the attempt if another woman pilot wanted to take the risk.

I knew about taking risks! And I had, at that time, completed 500 hours of solo flying. So when I was asked about the idea, I was ready to say yes!

On 17th June 1928, I *did* cross the Atlantic non-stop by air. But I wasn't alone. There were two other people in the aircraft. We flew from Newfoundland in Canada, to Wales in Britain. It took us 21 hours to complete the flight. I didn't fly the aircraft on that trip. I made notes about the flight while the others controlled the machine. But I made a decision. 'Next time, I'll be the pilot,' I told myself.

While I was in Britain, I bought another plane – an Avro Avian 594. And when I returned home, I toured the country talking about my flying experiences. A man

A Lockheed Vega aircraft. Amelia Earhart flew across the
Atlantic in one of these.

called G. P. Putnam <u>promoted</u> me as 'The Queen of
the Air'. He published books, but he also became the
<u>manager</u> of my flying career.

I became famous as a result of this tour. In fact, I
became a '<u>brand</u>'. One company named a brand of luggage
'Modernaire Earhart Luggage'. Another company gave
my name to a brand of clothes.

Soon, I and several other woman pilots started to
compete in air races. Some of the male pilots tried to make
this difficult for us. They stopped women competing in
several races. Perhaps they were jealous of our success.
My manager, G. P. Putnam, wasn't jealous. He asked me
to marry him several times. Finally I agreed and G.P. and
I were married on 7th February 1931.

◆ ◆ ◆

The next year, I was ready to make my solo attempt at
the Atlantic crossing. I was 34 years old. On 20th May 1932,

I <u>took off</u> from Harbour Grace in Newfoundland, and 15 hours later, I <u>landed</u> near Derry in Northern Ireland. I'd succeeded in my ambition – I was the first woman pilot to fly solo and non-stop across the Atlantic. As a result, the American government gave me a <u>medal</u> – the Distinguished Flying Cross. The French government gave me a medal too.

I attempted other records after that. I made the first solo flight from Hawaii to California, and then a flight from Los Angeles to Mexico City. And after that, I flew from Mexico to New York. 'Could a round-the-world trip be next?' I wondered. Other people had flown round the world, but I wanted to do it by the longest route. This meant following the equator – the widest part of the planet – for most of the journey.

In 1935, my husband and I moved from New York to California. G. P. left his job with his family's publishing company because he wanted to work for a film company in Hollywood. In California, I did some work at Purdue University, talking to women students about their careers, and supporting their ambitions. And the university decided to support *my* ambitions. People at the university helped to pay for my round-the-world record attempt.

A Lockheed 10 E Electra was the aircraft that I chose for this flight. The Lockheed Company put extra fuel containers in the aircraft for me, but this flight couldn't be non-stop. I needed to land for <u>refuelling</u> and rest in

The Distinguished Flying Cross

a lot of places. And I chose to take two <u>navigators</u> and an <u>engineer</u> with me on the flight. I wanted to fly the aircraft myself, but I needed to take people to help with <u>navigation</u> and repairs. I planned to leave these people at the refuelling-stops, and fly the last part of the journey alone.

In fact, my first attempt to fly round the world failed. The aircraft was damaged during <u>take-off</u> for the second stage of the flight. But it was possible to repair the damage, and on 1st June 1937, I set off again. This time, I took only one person with me – my navigator, Fred Noonan. We flew in stages to South America, to Africa, to India, to South-east Asia, and then to Australia. We'd completed 35,000 kilometres when we arrived in Lae, in Papua New Guinea.

On 2nd July 1937 we took off again. We were trying to reach Howland Island. From there, I planned to fly on to Hawaii, and then to California. Howland Island was only 2,000 metres long and 500 metres wide – it was like a tiny dot in the Pacific Ocean. And it was 5,000 kilometres from Lae.

An American Navy ship, the *Itasca*, was in the harbour at Howland Island. As we got near the island, the ship's crew heard our <u>radio signals</u>. They knew that we weren't far away, but they couldn't see us. Our aircraft was <u>running out of</u> fuel and we had to land *somewhere*, either on an island or in the sea. We hoped that our last radio message had been received. We hoped, but no help came.

The Life of Amelia Earhart

1897 Amelia Mary Earhart was born in Atchison, Kansas, on 24th July 1897.

1908 The family moved to Des Moines, Iowa. At the age of 11, Amelia saw her first aircraft.

1915 With her mother and sister, Amelia moved to Chicago.

1916 She left Hyde Park High School in Chicago and began Junior College at Ogontz School in Rydal, Pennslyvania.

1917 Amelia visited Toronto and trained as a nurse's assistant. She worked at the Spadina Military Hospital in Toronto, Canada.

1919 Amelia attended Columbia University for a year.

1920 On December 28th, Amelia flew for the first time, with a pilot called Frank Hawks.

1921 Amelia's first flying lesson was on 3rd January at Kinner Field near Long Beach. Later in the year, Amelia bought her first aircraft.

1922 Amelia flew her aircraft to an altitude of 4,300 metres, and set a world record for female pilots.

1923   On 15th May, she won her pilot's licence.

1925   She worked as a teacher, in Massachusetts.

1928–1929   Amelia was a member of a crew which flew across the Atlantic Ocean. She published a book called *20 Hours 40 Minutes*. She entered an air-race for the first time, and she came third.

1931   Amelia set women's speed records for 100-kilometre flights. She also set a world altitude record of 5,613 metres. She married George P. Putnam, her manager, on 7th February.

1932   On 20th May, Amelia became the first woman to fly solo across the Atlantic. The flight lasted 14 hours 56 minutes. In August, she also became the first woman to fly solo non-stop across the USA, coast to coast, from Los Angeles to Newark. She published *For the Fun of It*.

1933   Amelia competed in the National Air Races in Los Angeles, California. She broke her previous speed record for crossing America.

1935   Amelia became the first person to fly solo
        across the Pacific between Honolulu and
        Oakland, California. And she was the
        first person to fly solo non-stop from Los
        Angeles to Mexico City. Amelia joined the
        staff of Purdue University.

1937   Amelia attempted to fly round the world.
        During the attempt, she disappeared on
        2nd July 1937 at the age of 39. She was
        trying to find Howland Island and perhaps
        she crashed into the Pacific Ocean.

1939   Although her body was never found, the
        government decided that Amelia Earhart
        was dead on January 5th.

Amy Johnson

$\cdot \blacklozenge \cdot$

1903–1941

the British woman who broke records

I was one of the first British <u>competitive</u> woman pilots, and I broke many flying <u>records</u>. I became very famous. But an accident during the Second World War ended my life at the age of 37.

◆ ◆ ◆

My parents lived in the city of Hull, in England. I was born there on 1ˢᵗ July 1903. The year of my birth was an important one for aviation. Before 1903, people had been able to fly only in balloons and airships. Airships were like balloons with engines. But in 1903, <u>heavier-than-air</u> aeroplanes flew for the first time.

Those first aeroplanes didn't fly very far. And they flew in America and New Zealand – far from our home in Hull. But soon, people in Europe were building successful aeroplanes too. In 1909, Louis Blériot flew across the English Channel. Suddenly, the world was getting smaller!

My childhood was a happy one. My father was a <u>businessman</u> and my family had a lot of money. After attending school in Hull, I studied at Sheffield University. I enjoyed the parties and the dances. I enjoyed playing sports. But I also enjoyed studying for an <u>economics</u> degree. My ambition then was to become a <u>businesswoman</u>. So when I left the university in 1925, I took some courses in <u>business</u> studies. These courses and my degree gave me the skills to get a job in a financial company, and I quickly found one. I earned one pound a week, but I hated the job and I soon left.

Then, I fell in love for the first time. My parents didn't like my boyfriend. They made me an offer. They said I could take a long holiday in Canada. They wanted me to forget my boyfriend. I thought that they were wrong about him, so I didn't accept their offer. I stayed in England, but I soon decided that my parents were right about my boyfriend. I need to start my life again. So I decided to leave the north of England and live in London. I found a job with a law company there, and I soon learnt a lot about the law. I worked for that company for three years. For three years, I was the secretary of a lawyer called William Crocker. And for those three years, my life was very conventional. It was exactly like the lives of most other women from families like mine.

• ◆ •

Then, one day, everything changed for me. The weather was good that day. I decided to ride out of the city on a bus, and then take a walk. Soon, I was walking past an airfield. A large sign told me that it belonged to the London Aeroplane Club. Suddenly, I decided to find out about this club, so I walked in and looked for someone to talk to. I quickly discovered that all the members of the club were men. They were surprised to see a woman when I entered their clubroom. They were more surprised when I asked to join their club and to take flying lessons.

As soon as my lessons began, I knew that I had found what I wanted. My future was going to be in the air. I had to become a pilot.

• ◆ •

My first attempts at flying weren't very successful. My first teacher told me that I could never become a pilot. But I didn't give up my new ambition, and finally, I earned my licence in July 1929. By then, I was very interested in aeroplanes as machines. So I wanted a ground engineer's licence too – I wanted to repair aircraft as well as flying them. In December of the same year I earned a licence to work on engines. I was the first woman in Britain to have a ground engineer's licence.

Engineering and flying were not careers for women in 1930 – everyone said that. And women didn't travel alone between countries – everyone said that too. But my father was an unusual man and he didn't share these opinions. When I told him that I wanted to do all these things, he listened to me. The help that he gave me changed my life forever.

To start my new life, I needed an aeroplane. My father and a friend of his gave me some money. With this money I was able to buy a <u>second-hand</u> Gipsy Moth 60G, with a 100-<u>horsepower</u> engine. I named the little aeroplane *Jason*. Why? Because *Jason* was the <u>trademark</u> of my father's business.

So now I had my licences and an aeroplane. I was ready to fly. The question was, where could I fly to? Short journeys in England were easy, and flying to France wasn't difficult. I wanted to do something much more difficult, so I decided to fly to Australia, on my own.

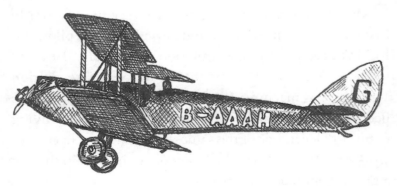

'Jason', the De Haviland Gypsy Moth aeroplane which
Amy Johnson flew to Australia

On 5th May 1930, I set out on my first solo flight between continents. Many people had warned me of the dangers of my plan. They'd reminded me that I had only 75 hours of flying experience. They'd asked me a lot of questions. How could I find airfields when I needed to <u>refuel</u>? How could I fly without getting lost? How could I stay on my <u>course</u> when I was tired and falling asleep? Could I <u>land</u> my aeroplane in the dark? Who could repair the aeroplane when it was damaged?

I wasn't scared by these questions – in fact they increased my wish to succeed. And when I left the ground on that day in May, I took only some simple maps with me in the small <u>cockpit</u> of my aeroplane.

My journey lasted 19 days, but nothing went seriously wrong. I flew over mountains and deserts. I flew through heavy rain and freezing cold winds. And once, I had to land in a sandstorm. I stopped to refuel in some very small places, and the people in them had never seen an aeroplane with a woman pilot. My route also allowed me refuelling-stops at big British-owned airfields in India and Singapore. And finally, on 24th May, *Jason* arrived in the Australian city of Darwin.

I had flown 18,600 kilometres. The people of Darwin were surprised to see me, but they gave me a good welcome. I'd hoped to beat Bert Hinkler's speed record for an England-to-Australia solo flight, but I'd been too slow. I hadn't broken that record, but I *had* <u>established</u> a new one. I

Amy Johnson's route to Australia

was the first woman to fly solo from Britain to Australia. I was pleased about that. And I was pleased that the *Daily Mail* newspaper had given me £10,000 to celebrate my flight.

◆ ◆ ◆

I'd established one new record. Now I wanted to break some other records and I became very competitive. A year after my Australian flight, I set off from London to fly to Moscow, in Russia. This time I wasn't alone, I had a <u>co-pilot</u> – a man called Jack Humphreys. We flew in a Puss Moth aeroplane. It took us 21 hours to fly the distance of 2,830 kilometres. This was the first time the flight had been completed in less than a day – another new record.

After a short rest, we continued on across Siberia. This was a huge region, with very few people in it. We had to choose our stops carefully, between the <u>tundra</u> and mountains. And after Siberia, we flew on to Tokyo, in Japan. Again, we broke the England–Japan speed record.

◆ ◆ ◆

On my return to Britain, I met Jim Mollison. Jim, who came from Scotland, was also a record-breaking aviator. A few hours after our first meeting, he asked me to marry him. We were flying together at the time. The British newspapers called us 'The Flying <u>Sweethearts</u>'. And on 29th July 1932, we were married.

Soon afterwards, I flew solo to Cape Town, in South Africa. In the Puss Moth, the journey took four days and seven hours – a new record. This time, the record which I broke had been established by my own husband!

In February 1933, I was happy to receive an <u>honour</u>. I was given the Segrave Trophy for aviation. And soon after that, Jim and I flew together again. We made a non-stop flight from Wales, in the west of Britain, to the USA. The aeroplane this time was a De Havilland Dragon Rapide. We reached the USA, but we <u>ran out of</u> fuel before we could land at an airfield. We crashed into the ground at Bridgeport, Connecticut. We were both hurt, but not very badly. The flight made us famous in America. People in New York, and in Atlantic City, gave us a wonderful welcome.

When we got back to England, I started on a new career. I began to sell aeroplanes for a company which built them. But soon there were other flights to make and other records to break. I still spent much of my time in the air.

In 1934, Jim and I flew to India. We were in a race to reach Australia. An engine problem stopped us in Allahabad. We couldn't continue to Australia but we had established a new record for a Britain-to-India flight.

After my flight in 1932, another pilot had broken my Britain-to-South Africa record. But in 1936, I won it again. This was my last record-breaking flight.

In the years before the Second World War, I was a famous person – a celebrity. A composer, Horatio Nicholls, wrote a popular song about me called 'Amy, Wonderful Amy', and several well-known singers recorded it. My photograph was often in the newspapers. It was a tiring life, but a happy one most of the time. One thing made me sad. After six years of marriage, Jim and I decided we didn't want to be together any more. I stopped using the name Amy Mollison and I became Amy Johnson again.

◆ ◆ ◆

When the war started, in 1939, I joined the Air Transport Auxiliary. This was a group of pilots which included many women. We worked with the British Royal Air Force. Many new aeroplanes were built each week. Our job was to fly them from the factories to the military airfields where they were needed. Although women weren't allowed to fly into battle, this was important war work too.

On 5th January 1941, I was asked to fly an aeroplane from Blackpool to Oxford. It was quite a short distance for someone with my history. But that flight was my last. The weather over England that day was really bad, and I became lost. I flew much too far east. I ran out of fuel, and my aeroplane crashed into the wide mouth of the river Thames. I died in the very cold water.

The Life of Amy Johnson

1903   Amy Johnson was born in Hull, in England. As a young woman, she earned a degree in economics from the University of Sheffield.

1929   Amy lived and worked in London. For three years, she was the secretary of a lawyer called William Crocker. During this time, she started flying lessons and earned a pilot's licence. She became the first British woman to earn a ground engineer's licence.

1930   She was the first woman to fly solo from England to Australia. She received the Harmon Trophy.

1931   Amy and her co-pilot, Jack Humphreys, became the first pilots to fly from London to Moscow in one day.

1932   Amy met and married the Scottish pilot, Jim Mollison. Amy established a solo record for the flight from London to Cape Town, in South Africa.

1933   Amy and Jim flew non-stop from Pendine Sands in South Wales to the USA. Their aeroplane ran out of fuel and crashed in Connecticut. They were both hurt, but not very badly. In this year, Amy was given the Segrave Trophy for aviation.

1934   The couple made another long-distance flight together, from Britain to India. This flight was part of a race from Britain to Australia. Amy and Jim didn't complete the flight because of an engine problem. But they *did* establish a new Britain-to-India record.

1935   In this year, Amy became the President of the Women's Engineering Society. She had this position for two years.

1936   Amy made her last record-breaking flight from Britain to South Africa. Another pilot had broken her 1932 record for this journey. But now, Amy got the record again.

1938   Amy and Jim's marriage ended and Amy used the name Johnson again, instead of Mollison.

1940   During the Second World War, Amy joined the Air Transport Auxiliary, and transported Royal Air Force aircraft from factories to airfields.

1941   Amy died in the River Thames, aged 37, after running out of fuel during a flight for the Air Transport Auxiliary.

♦ GLOSSARY ♦

altitude NOUN
a measurement of height above
the level of the sea

ascend VERB
to move upwards

brand NOUN
the name of a product that a
particular company makes

business NOUN
an organization that produces
and sells goods or that provides
a service

businessman (businessmen)
NOUN
a man who works in business

**businesswoman
(businesswomen)** NOUN
a woman who works in business

cloth UNCOUNTABLE NOUN
material that is used for making
clothing

cockpit NOUN
the part of an aeroplane where
the pilot sits

compartment NOUN
one of the separate sections of
something

competitive ADJECTIVE
competing with other people
or groups

co-pilot NOUN
a pilot who helps the main pilot
in an aeroplane

course NOUN
the direction in which someone
or something is going

criminal NOUN
a person who does something
illegal

cubic metre NOUN
a unit of volume that is one metre
long on each side

demonstrate VERB
to show people how something
works or how to do something

demonstration NOUN
a talk by someone who shows
you how to do something or
how something works

display NOUN
an event in which something is
presented to the public in order
to entertain or impress them

dream NOUN
something that you often think about because you would like it to happen
VERB
to see events in your mind while you are asleep

dreamer NOUN
someone who looks forward to pleasant things that may never happen, rather than being realistic and practical

economics UNCOUNTABLE NOUN
the study of the way in which money and industry are organized in a society

engineer NOUN
a person who designs, builds and repairs machines, or structures such as roads and bridges

engineering UNCOUNTABLE NOUN
the work of designing and building machines or structures such as roads and bridges

establish VERB
to create something new, for example an organization

experiment NOUN
a scientific test that you do in order to discover what happens to something

fixed-wing ADJECTIVE
having wings that stay in a fixed position rather than ones that move

fog UNCOUNTABLE NOUN
thick cloud that is close to the ground

headlamp NOUN
one of the two large powerful lights at the front of a vehicle

heavier-than-air ADJECTIVE
used for describing flying machines, as opposed to balloons

hobby NOUN
an activity that you enjoy doing in your free time

honour NOUN
something special that someone is allowed to do

horsepower UNCOUNTABLE NOUN
a unit of power used for measuring how powerful an engine is

iceberg NOUN
a very large piece of ice that floats in the sea

infect VERB
to affect a person or part of their body so that they become ill

invade VERB
to attack and enter a country

invent VERB
to be the first person to think of something or to make it

invention NOUN
something that has been invented by someone

inventor NOUN
someone who has invented something, or whose job is to invent things

invest VERB
to put money into a business or a bank, in order to try to make a profit from it

kidnap VERB
to take someone away by force and keep them as a prisoner, often until their friends or family pay a large amount of money

land VERB
to bring a plane or spacecraft to the ground at the end of a journey

manager NOUN
a person who controls all or part of a business or organization

map VERB
to make a map of an area or route

mapping UNCOUNTABLE NOUN
the activity of making a map of an area or route

medal NOUN
a small metal disc that you receive as a prize for doing something very good

monoplane NOUN
an aeroplane with one set of wings, rather than two or three sets

movement NOUN
when something changes position, or goes from one place to another

navigation UNCOUNTABLE NOUN
the job or activity of working out the direction in which an aircraft should be travelling

navigator NOUN
the person on an aircraft whose job is to work out the direction in which it should be travelling

parachute NOUN
a large piece of thin material that a person attaches to their body when they jump from an aircraft to help them float safely to the ground

passenger NOUN
someone who is travelling in a
vehicle but is not driving it

pleasure-flight NOUN
a trip in an aircraft taken for
pleasure rather than simply to
get from one place to another

practical ADJECTIVE
sensible and able to deal
effectively with problems

promote VERB
to help to make something
successful

radio signal NOUN
a sound sent by radio waves that
gives a message to someone

record NOUN
the best result ever in a particular
sport or activity

refuel VERB
to put more fuel in an aircraft or
other vehicle so that it can
continue its journey

refuelling UNCOUNTABLE NOUN
the process of putting more fuel
in an aircraft or other vehicle so
that it can continue its journey
ADJECTIVE relating to the process
of putting more fuel in an aircraft
or other vehicle so that it can
continue its journey

reserve NOUN
a group of soldiers who are
ready to join a military operation
if they are needed but are not
full-time soldiers

retire VERB
to leave your job and stop
working completely

retirement UNCOUNTABLE NOUN
the period in someone's life after
they retire

revolution NOUN
an attempt by a group of people
to change their country's
government by using force

risk NOUN
something you do that might
have a bad result

rope NOUN
a type of very thick string that is
made by twisting together
several strings or wires

run out of PHRASAL VERB
to have no more of something
left

second-hand ADJECTIVE
not new but already used by
another person

sinus NOUN
one of the two spaces in the
bone behind your nose

speech NOUN
a formal talk that someone gives to a group of people

stable ADJECTIVE
not likely to wobble or fall

stand NOUN
an object designed to put something on

surgery UNCOUNTABLE NOUN
a process in which a doctor cuts open a patient's body in order to repair, remove or replace a diseased or damaged part

survival UNCOUNTABLE NOUN
when someone or something still exists after a difficult or dangerous time

sweetheart NOUN
your boyfriend or girlfriend

take off PHRASAL VERB
to leave the ground and start flying

take-off NOUN
the time when a plane leaves the ground and starts flying

telegraph wires NOUN
overhead wires used for sending messages over long distances

trademark NOUN
a special name or symbol that a company owns and uses on its products

tundra NOUN
one of the large, flat, cold areas of land in the north of Europe, Asia, and America

unstable ADJECTIVE
likely to wobble or fall

wire NOUN
a long thin piece of metal

zodiac UNCOUNTABLE NOUN
a diagram representing the positions of the planets and stars that is divided into twelve sections, each with a special name and symbol

Collins
English Readers

ALSO AVAILABLE IN THE AMAZING PEOPLE READERS SERIES:

Level 1

Amazing Leaders
978-0-00-754492-9
William the Conqueror, Saladin, Genghis Khan, Catherine the Great, Abraham Lincoln, Queen Victoria

Amazing Inventors
978-0-00-754494-3
Johannes Gutenberg, Louis Braille, Alexander Graham Bell, Thomas Edison, Guglielmo Marconi, John Logie Baird

Amazing Entrepreneurs and Business People *(May 2014)*
978-0-00-754501-8
Mayer Rothschild, Cornelius Vanderbilt, Will Kellogg, Elizabeth Arden, Walt Disney, Soichiro Honda

Amazing Women *(May 2014)*
978-0-00-754493-6
Harriet Tubman, Emmeline Pankhurst, Maria Montessori, Hellen Keller, Nancy Wake, Eva Peron

Amazing Performers *(June 2014)*
978-0-00-754508-7
Glenn Miller, Perez Prado, Ella Fitzgerald, Luciano Pavarotti, John Lennon

Level 2

Amazing Architects and Artists
978-0-00-754496-7
Leonardo da Vinci, Christopher Wren, Antoni Gaudí, Pablo Picasso, Frida Kahlo

Amazing Composers *(May 2014)*
978-0-00-754502-5
JS Bach, Wolfgang Mozart, Giuseppe Verdi, Johann Strauss, Pyotr Tchaikovsky, Irving Berlin

Amazing Mathematicians *(May 2014)*
978-0-00-754503-2
Galileo Galilei, René Descartes, Isaac Newton, Carl Gauss, Charles Babbage, Ada Lovelace

Amazing Medical People *(June 2014)*
978-0-00-754509-4
Edward Jenner, Florence Nightingale, Elizabeth Garrett, Carl Jung, Jonas Salk, Christiaan Barnard

Level 3

Amazing Explorers
978-0-00-754497-4
Marco Polo, Ibn Battuta, Christopher Columbus, James Cook, David Livingstone, Yuri Gagarin

Amazing Writers
978-0-00-754498-1
Geoffrey Chaucer, William Shakespeare, Charles Dickens, Victor Hugo, Leo Tolstoy, Rudyard Kipling

Amazing Philanthropists
(May 2014)
978-0-00-754504-9
Alfred Nobel, Andrew Carnegie, John Rockefeller, Thomas Barnardo, Henry Wellcome, Madam CJ Walker

Amazing Performers *(June 2014)*
978-0-00-754505-6
Pablo Casals, Louis Armstrong, Édith Piaf, Frank Sinatra, Maria Callas, Elvis Presley

Amazing Scientists *(June 2014)*
978-0-00-754510-0
Antoine Lavoisier, Humphry Davy, Gregor Mendel, Louis Pasteur, Charles Darwin, Francis Crick

Level 4

Amazing Thinkers and Humanitarians
978-0-00-754499-8
Confucius, Socrates, Aristotle, William Wilberforce, Karl Marx, Mahatma Gandhi

Amazing Scientists
978-0-00-754500-1
Alessandro Volta, Michael Faraday, Marie Curie, Albert Einstein, Alexander Fleming, Linus Pauling

Amazing Writers *(May 2014)*
978-0-00-754506-3
Voltaire, Charlotte Brontë, Mark Twain, Jacques Prevert, Ayn Rand, Aleksandr Solzhenitsyn

Amazing Leaders *(May 2014)*
978-0-00-754507-0
Julius Caesar, Queen Elizabeth I, George Washington, King Louis XVI, Winston Churchill, Che Guevara

Amazing Entrepreneurs and Business People *(June 2014)*
978-0-00-754511-7
Henry Heinz, William Lever, Michael Marks, Henry Ford, Coco Chanel, Ray Kroc